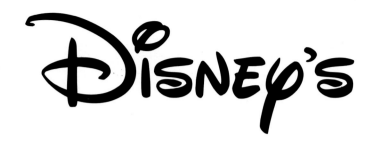

HYPERION

NEW YORK

PHOTOMOSAICS™

Robert Silvers
Text by Robert Tieman

Photomosaic™ is a trademark of Runaway Technologies, Inc.

To contact the author, or for more information on Photomosaics,
please visit www.photomosaic.com.

ISBN 0-7868-6463-X

Book design by Christine Weathersbee

First Edition
10 9 8 7 6 5 4 3 2 1
Printed in Japan

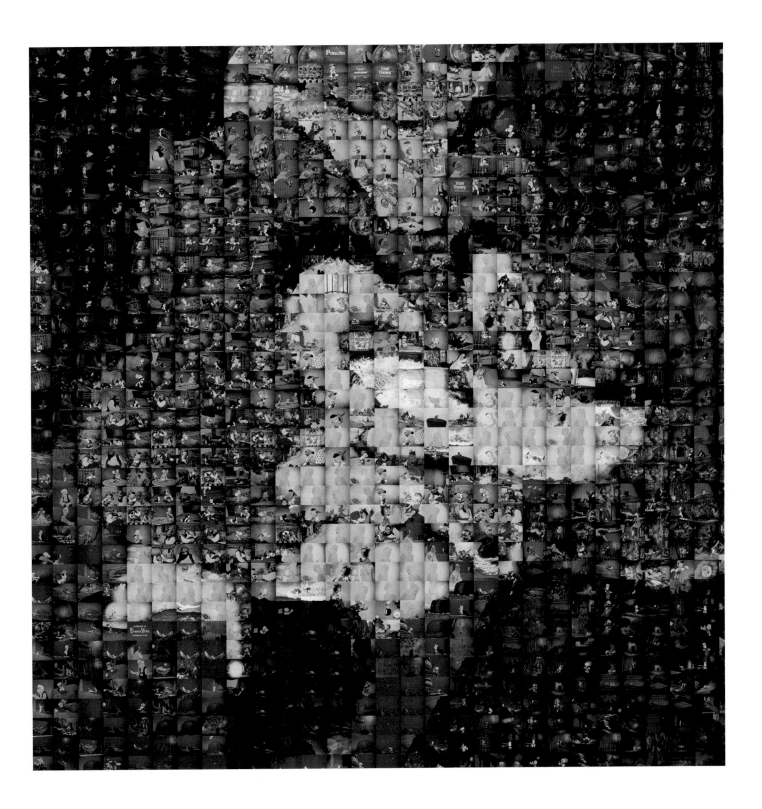

Introduction

If a picture is worth a thousand words, what about thousands of pictures? What if those pictures are not just randomly selected but rather are carefully chosen and arranged elements of a new vocabulary? In an attempt to answer these questions, I have selected tens of thousands of elements from many of Disney's wonderful animated films to represent my favorite Disney moments. I call these arrangements Photomosaics.

Photomosaics are my unique medium for visually telling a story. Because these mosaics are made from images rather than solid colored tiles, the messages are conveyed on more than one level. There is a relationship between everything you see. Look from afar and view the overall subject. Come up close and discover unexpected treasures. This is not unlike the world itself. Look at the Earth from space and it forms a beautiful image. Now come in close and see all the people, animals, and other unanticipated and exciting characters existing in harmony. Each element is complex and can be seen on many levels. What I have tried to accomplish with *Disney's Photomosaics*™ is to create images that reveal more and more as you investigate them more closely. I loved using the world of Disney as my palette for this new medium. Thank you, and I hope you enjoy them.

Robert Silvers
www.photomosaic.com

MICKEY MOUSE

1928

"I often find myself surprised at what has been said about our redoubtable little Mickey who was never really a mouse nor yet wholly a man, although always recognizably human. The psychoanalysts have probed him. Wise men of critical inclination have pondered him. Columnists have kidded him. Admirers have saluted him in extravagant terms. . . . But all we ever intended for him and expected of him was that he should continue to make people everywhere chuckle with him and at him." —Walt Disney

SNOW WHITE

1937

Under the category of "Out of the Mouths of Babes" came the report of a movie studio executive who took his 4 ½-year-old daughter to see *Snow White and the Seven Dwarfs* shortly after it had premiered in Los Angeles. The girl pronounced the movie as okay, but one thing troubled her. Why, she asked her father, did the Wicked Queen change herself into a horrid old witch?

The father explained that the Queen wanted to destroy Snow White, because she was more beautiful than she, and that the Queen used magic to create an ugly disguise for herself.

The little girl just shook her head and said, "If she could do that, why didn't she just change herself into a more beautiful Queen?"

Uh. Time for bed, dear.

PINOCCHIO

1940

*"Little puppet made of pine,
Wake! The gift of life is thine."*

Movie audiences noticed a more lifelike quality to Walt Disney's second animated feature. The cel painters developed a technique known as "the blend" which utilized subtle shading on skin and costumes, giving a rounder appearance to faces and bodies. Improvements were also made to the Studio's multiplane camera, allowing an increased depth of focus. And significant advancements in the Effects Department enhanced the illusion of life—from the glow of a candle flame to the transparency of the water in a fishbowl to the glitter and sparkle of a wishing star.

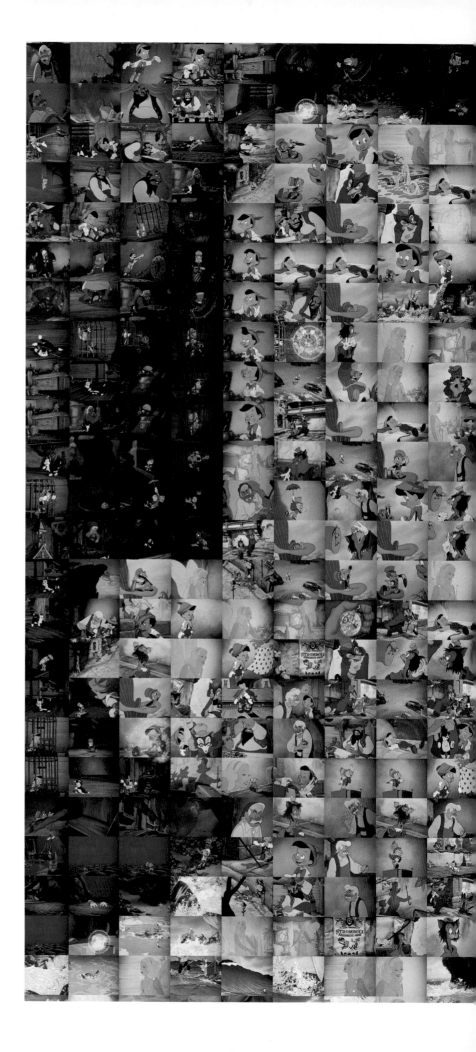

FANTASIA

1940

Fantasia, Walt Disney's experiment in sight and sound in 1940, had something for everyone . . . to complain about. A prominent critic for the *New York Herald Tribune* wrote: "I left the theater in a condition bordering on nervous breakdown." Another said, "A woman next to me wept—and not for joy, either."

Throughout his career, Walt didn't much care what critics thought, had always insisted that he made his films for the general audience to appreciate. The original failure of *Fantasia*, however, seemed to stick with him.

When asked about it in 1964, he was somewhat philosophical. "Some of the critics said, "Why does Disney have to put pictures to music. Can't we just sit and listen to music and make our own pictures?"

"But there is a great segment of that audience, that by seeing the pictures to *Fantasia* became acquainted with some of this classical music. And it even led to them becoming interested in other classics . . . in getting them excited . . . So I think we made a contribution, but you can never please the purists."

DUMBO

1941

Technicolor pachyderms

After Dumbo innocently took a drink of champagne-spiked water, he experienced the wild and surreal delirium of Pink Elephants on Parade, one of the more celebrated pieces of animation to come out of the Disney studio.

"We have a good start on something crazy here and I believe we should keep it crazy," said Walt during a story conference. "I can see those polka dots doing a swell dance. You could use plaids and things. Blue stripes and red stripes...I like that gingham effect." He even encouraged the animators to play with paperdolls on company time.

In order to create many of the fantastical forms and patterns seen in the Pink Elephants sequence, the animators took scissors to folded paper and cut out variously shaped elephants. By unfolding the resulting string of figures they were able to create far stranger combinations faster than they could draw them.

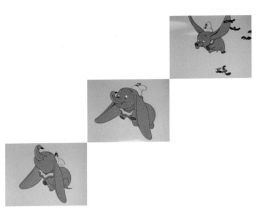

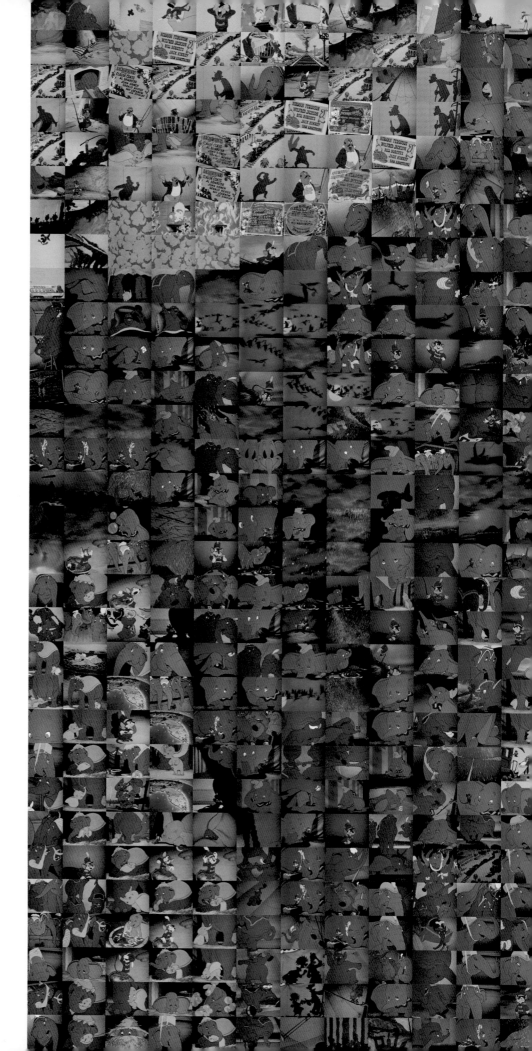

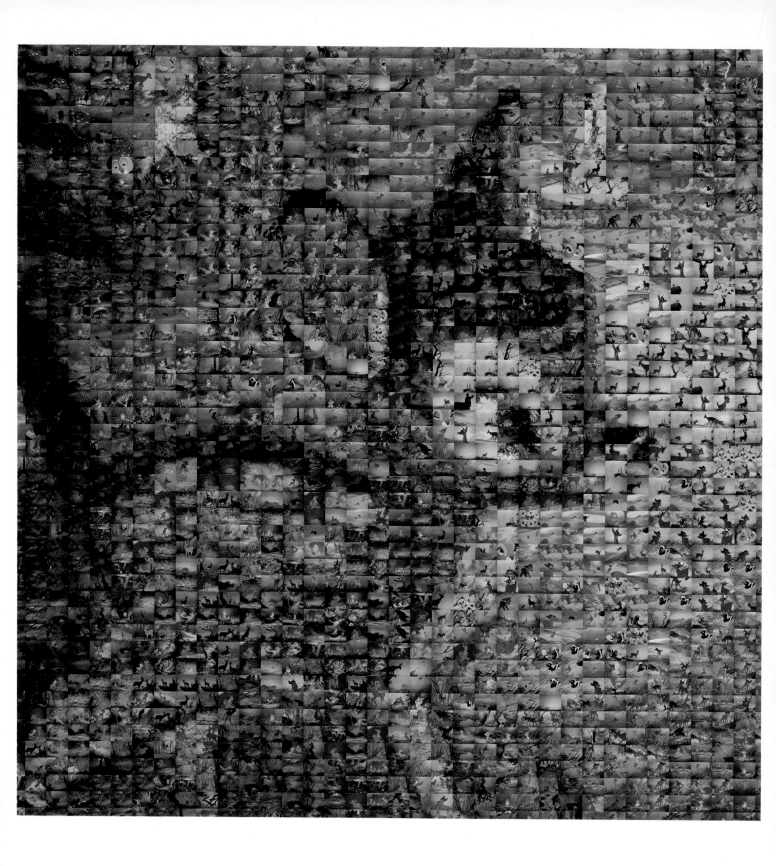

BAMBI

1942

Bambi is not so much a narrative story, but more a collection of scenes in the young deer's life. Disney animators Frank Thomas and Ollie Johnston called it "a mosaic of isolated adventures."

In *Bambi*, Walt Disney and his artists achieved the perfect synthesis of utter realism in the anatomical correctness of the animals and painterly impressionism in the lush, poetic backgrounds of the forest. More so than any of his films, here he combined the storytelling elements of visual character development, musical score as something of a Greek chorus, unparalleled effects animation, humor, and tragedy—all told from the animals' point of view *and* with fewer than 1500 words of spoken dialogue.

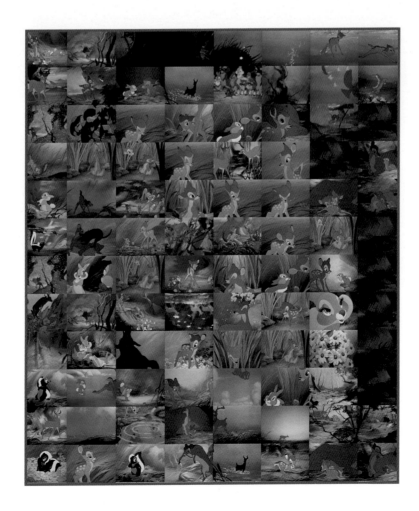

CINDERELLA

1950

Not just anyone could write "Salaga doola menchika boola." Songwriters Mack David and Jerry Livingston were asked to come up with a song for the Fairy Godmother when she turns the pumpkin into the coach for Cinderella's night at the ball. They needed lyrics that would suggest the mumbo jumbo of magic, but didn't want to use the usual incantations "abracadabra" or "hocus pocus." Instead, they searched for nonsense words with a good rhythm that could go along with the rolling of the coach on the road to the castle.

After two weeks of head scratching and 30 or 40 discarded combinations, the first two lines and the accompanying melody just rolled out. It took only one more day to finish the song and "Bibbidi-Bobbidi-Boo" went on to the Hit Parade, dozens of recordings by the top singers of the day, and an Academy Award® nomination for Best Song.

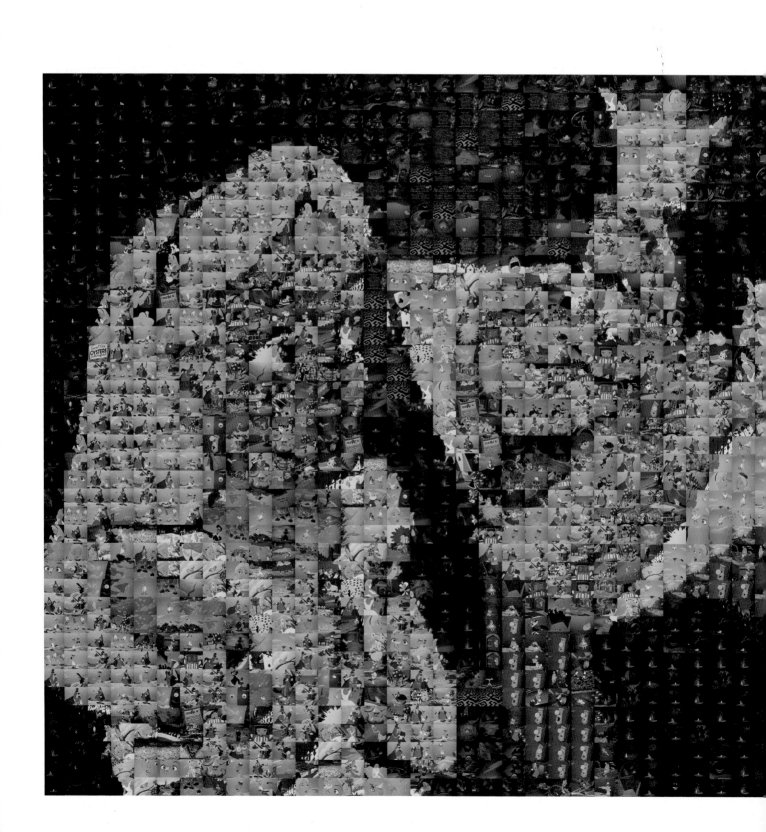

ALICE IN WONDERLAND

1951

Alice in Wonderland was the first Disney animated feature to have its film frames translated into pixels for the TV screen.

While the other Hollywood studio chiefs initially viewed television as a competitor, Walt Disney quickly recognized the value of the new medium and its possibilities as a promotional tool. On Christmas Day, 1950, he ventured into television production for the first time, with an NBC special entitled "One Hour in Wonderland." Showing a few film clips from the not-yet-released *Alice*, Walt hoped to whet the appetites of the audience. He succeeded far beyond his expectations. The program was seen by 90% of the available audience.

By 1954, Walt began production of his weekly *Disneyland* anthology series for ABC. Originally, feature films were not part of the deal, but he and ABC realized they would be a tremendous draw. "Alice in Wonderland" was the second episode broadcast that first year and was #1 in the ratings that evening.

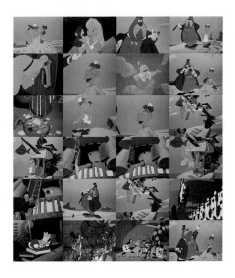

PETER PAN

1953

Peter Pan—a boy at last.

After half a century of life in various stage versions, Peter Pan's genuine boyishness was first revealed to audiences in Walt Disney's animated version of James M. Barrie's famous fantasy. The role of the boy who wouldn't grow up had been traditionally played by a woman—most famously by theater legends Maude Adams and Mary Martin, most recently by gymnast Cathy Rigby. Walt broke with tradition, not only by having Peter drawn as a real boy, but also using the vocal talents of one of his favorite young male stars, Bobby Driscoll (*Song of the South* and *Treasure Island*).

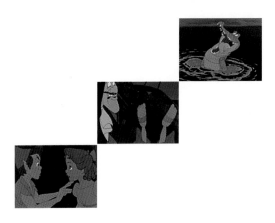

LADY AND THE TRAMP

1955

Released in 1955, *Lady and the Tramp* was another first in Walt Disney's long list of pioneering accomplishments in motion pictures—the first full-length animated film in CinemaScope™. This wide-screen process, introduced in 1953, was primarily used to display grand vistas of scenery and spectacle.

"Visually, CinemaScope gave us the opportunity—indeed, the necessity—to experiment with action, groupings and setting," Walt said. "And we were able to do more in our backgrounds and settings because we had a larger canvas on which to work."

In the regular screen format, it was relatively easy for a single animated character to enliven the whole screen. When the characters were grouped in a scene, they were close together and easier for the animators to handle. CinemaScope required that the painted backgrounds be much more carefully composed and that the characters in a scene be dispersed. More long shots and extended pans were used to show off the medium. This doubled, and even tripled, the amount of work for the artists, increasing expenses by as much as 30% over a regular animated feature.

Even the size of the paper used by the animators was larger in many scenes. All the drawings, laid end to end, would stretch more than 4 million feet, or more than 750 miles.

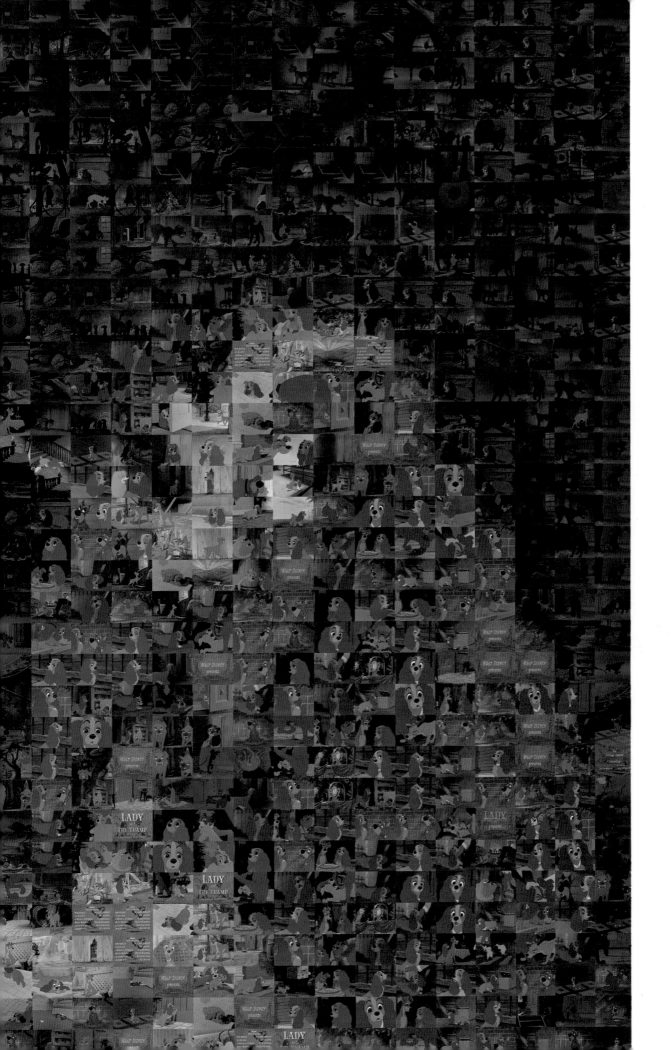

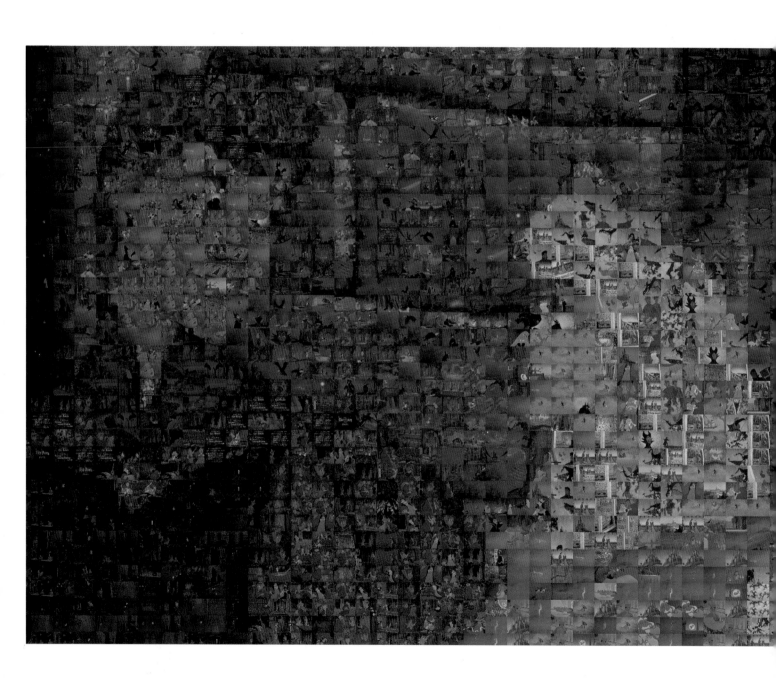

SLEEPING BEAUTY

1959

The castle doors blast open. A ferocious wind whips the flowing robes of King Stefan and his Queen. Lightning and thunder strike terror in the faces of the assembled crowd. The ceremonial hall grows dark and the evil fairy Maleficent appears amid a burst of flames.

At a special screening of *Sleeping Beauty* held for executives of Dupont and their families, most of the parents leaned over in their seats at this point to comfort their children who were screaming in fright at the dramatic and flamboyant appearance of Maleficent.

One set of parents, however, sat dumbstruck as their little boy Brad gazed at the screen in rapt attention, clapping his hands with glee. His father leaned across the boy and said to the mother, "We're going to have trouble with this one."

101 DALMATIANS

1961

Walt Disney, Ub Iwerks and The Haloid Company

The Haloid Company??

Better known by its modern name (Xerox Corporation), Haloid of Rochester, NY, had invented something called xerography, heralded at the time as "a clean, fast, dry direct positive, electrostatic copying process."

Ub Iwerks, the original animator of Mickey Mouse, was the Disney Studio's director of technical research in the 1950s. He began experimenting with xerography and in 1959 successfully modified a Xerox camera to transfer the animators' original pencil drawings directly onto cels. This not only saved time and money, but it also preserved the spontaneity and individual artistic touches that came from the animators' pencils.

For years to come, the new process had a significant and defining effect on the way Disney animation would look. The distinctive line of the cels influenced the art direction and the painted backgrounds so that the styles of the characters and their settings wouldn't clash. It gave a very graphic and linear look to the films that was quite different than the earlier movies.

In addition, the creative challenge of animating dozens of puppies in the same scene could not have even been contemplated without the ability to copy the drawings, not to mention all those spots—some 6,469,952 of them!

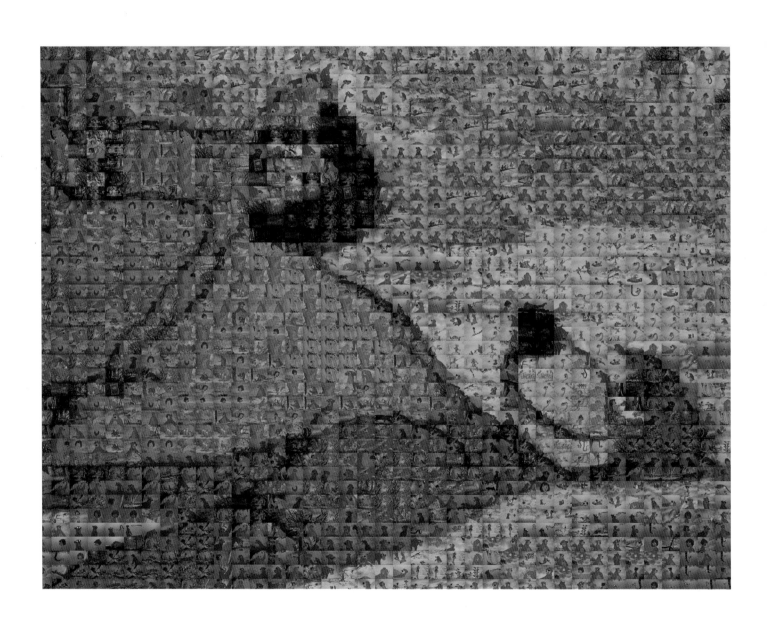

THE JUNGLE BOOK

1967

Over the years, people often asked Walt Disney where he got his ideas for stories. Some of the best came from classic fairy tales, others adapted from books. When it came time to tackle Rudyard Kipling's *The Jungle Book*, the story team felt the source material was too much a collection of dark, disjointed chapters, with no continuity. Walt assigned Larry Clemmons to write the animated feature with the admonishment, "First thing I want you to do is *not* read the book."

Walt repeated this to Richard and Robert Sherman, the songwriters for the movie. "I don't ever want you to read it. This is a story about a kid who gets raised by wolves and he's brought back to a village. That's the basic story line . . . and we wanna have fun with it." That sense of fun permeated the entire production of *The Jungle Book* and the result was the jazziest jungle movie ever.

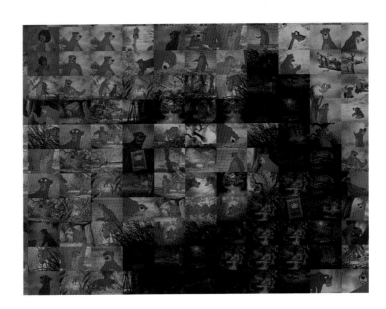

MANY ADVENTURES OF WINNIE THE POOH

1977

Walt Disney first expressed a desire to purchase the rights to A.A. Milne's *Winnie-the-Pooh* in 1937 (in spite of the dire assessments of his Story Department). The deal was hindered by the fact that someone else had signed up certain merchandising rights. In 1941, and again in 1945, further attempts to acquire the property were made, and failed. ("Oh, bother!")

Walt was finally able to close a deal in 1961, and a "Winnie the Pooh" full-length animated film was put into production. Three years later, however, the project was being reevaluated with serious questions of whether the slight story could hold up as a feature. The Studio decided to release the first portion of the story as a featurette, with the possibility of other Pooh stories of similar lengths being made in the future. A 1964 memo recommended waiting "for development of subsequent segments, and then at a later date package them together as a feature theatrical project."

Winnie the Pooh and the Honey Tree (1966) was followed by *Winnie the Pooh and the Blustery Day* (1968) and *Winnie the Pooh and Tigger Too* (1974). The combined feature finally appeared—nearly 40 years after the original inquiries were made—in 1977.

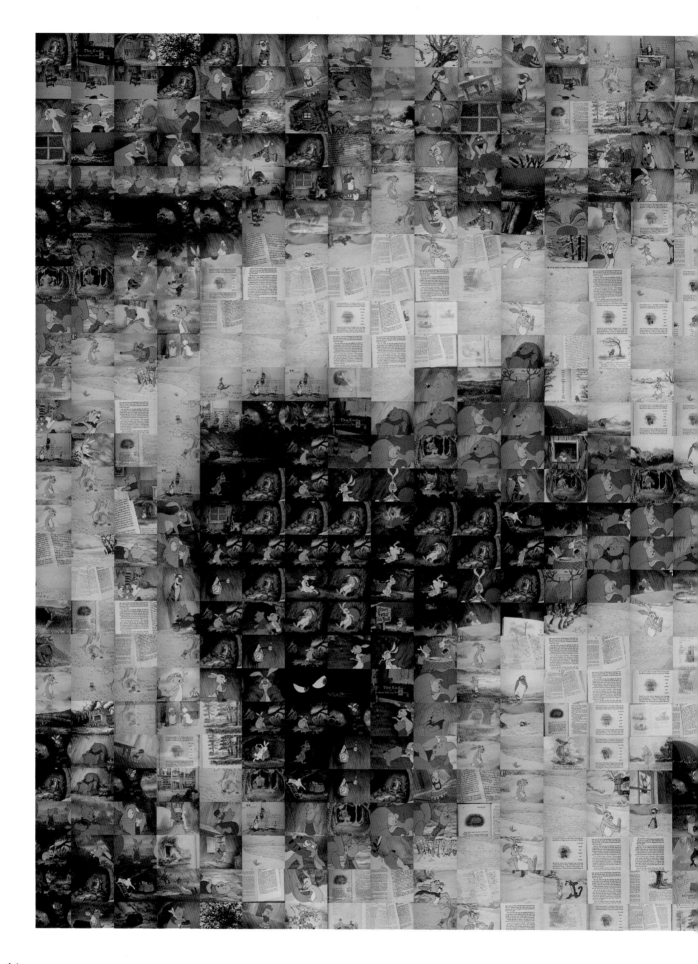

THE LITTLE MERMAID

1989

Disney artists—both in animation and in theme park architecture—often include in their designs what have come to be known as "hidden Mickeys." By looking carefully at the rockwork, for instance, in a Walt Disney World resort fireplace, one can spot the famous outline of Mickey Mouse's head. But "under the sea"?!

Looking carefully at the assembled audience when King Triton makes his grand entrance, Mickey Mouse, Donald Duck, and Goofy are sitting together in one row. Kermit the Frog can be spotted a few rows back, and several merpeople in the crowd sport Mickey Mouse ears.

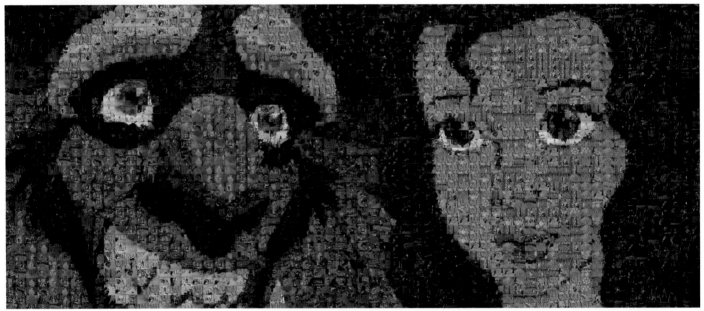

BEAUTY AND THE BEAST

1991

A few months before the theatrical premiere of *Beauty and the Beast*, Disney presented a work-in-progress version of the film at the New York Film Festival. This unfinished edition was a step by step demonstration on how an animated feature is created. The presentation consisted of about two-thirds finished color footage, along with story sketches, rough pencil animation, and cleaned up drawings.

The critics raved, with the *New York Times* calling the work in progress "a revelation, particularly for viewers who grew up watching animated films and have come to feel blasé about them."

This "special edition" of *Beauty and the Beast* was so impressive the Studio took the unprecedented move of releasing it on laser disc for a wider audience to appreciate. The following year, the finished film went on to make further Hollywood history by becoming the first animated film ever to be nominated for a Best Picture Academy Award®.

ALADDIN
1992

The first animator assigned to *Aladdin*, Eric Goldberg decided early on to take his inspiration for the Genie from famed caricaturist Al Hirschfeld. Using a minimum of lines to illustrate a curvy swirl of smoke with a face, a strong personality for the Genie emerged and Goldberg ran with it. His sense of design then influenced the entire film. The swooping lines and the S-curves of Arabic calligraphy unified the characters and seeped into the backgrounds, giving the whole film a fluidity so different from what Disney animation had been before. According to Goldberg, the goal was "to simplify forms to their organic shapes ... to give the animators a lot of freedom of draftsmanship so they can make their performances that much richer and expressive."

TIM BURTON'S THE NIGHTMARE BEFORE CHRISTMAS

1993

Tim Burton had wanted to make this movie ever since he worked as an animator at Disney in the early 1980s. Very early on, he wanted it to be made using the challenging technique of stop-motion animation—the filming of 3-dimensional models, one frame at a time, with minute changes in their pose.

All moving pictures, even those with live actors, are actually still pictures—24 distinct photographs every second. Run through a projector, or in a flip book, the human brain merges the separate images into a continuous illusion of movement by a phenomenon known as persistence of vision. String a couple hundred thousand of these individual pictures together and you've got a full length movie.

THE LION KING

1994

For Disney animation, voice talent is recorded first and then animators bring the characters to life on paper. Supervising animators for Timon and Pumbaa—Tony Bancroft and Mike Surrey—had fun working with Nathan Lane and Ernie Sabella, who are friends off-screen as well. Surrey joked, "In real life, the warthog would probably eat the meerkat, so we've obviously taken quite a few liberties in making them best friends. With these two characters, we were able to go much broader and concentrate mainly on their personalities."

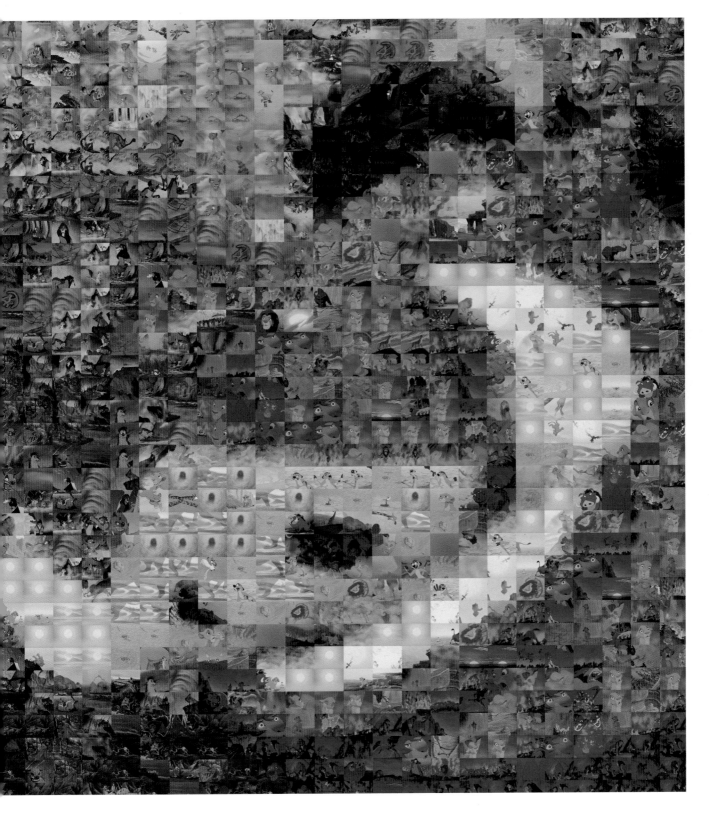

TOY STORY

1995

Toy Story represented a milestone in animated moviemaking as the first fulllength feature to be created wholly by artists using computer tools and technology. Just as Robert Silvers did to create his Photomosaics technique, so did the computer wizards at Pixar animation studio have to write and perfect their own proprietary software in order to create the very believable world where toys have a life of their own.

The artists in both cases, with their computers, create a unique look with unrivaled qualities of color, texture, light, and detail, whether for the individual frames of a 77-minute film or the 1,600 photo "tiles" of this mosaic.

To infinity and beyond.

HERCULES

1997

Advancing the art of animation continued as a Disney tradition with *Hercules*. The directors of the film envisioned Olympus, the home of the gods, as a city actually made of clouds. The challenge became creating such an effect on the screen.

Three-dimensional clouds were considered, but discarded as being too jarring when combined with the traditional handpainted backgrounds of the skies. The solution was found in a live action special effects method: morphing—a bit of trickery involving multiple dissolves where one image turns into the next.

The computer graphics artists had to design their own sophisticated morphing program. By using a small series of painted key cloud "poses," they were able to create a breathtaking city of living, breathing clouds that the gods could transform into other objects at will.